TRADING
LOGBOOK

_____

_____

_____

TRADING LOGBOOK ⇄

Rules No.

Rules No.

Rules No.

Rules No.

TRADING LOGBOOK ⇄

Rules No.

Rules No.

Rules No.

Rules No.

TRADING LOGBOOK ⇆

Rules No.

Rules No.

Rules No.

Rules No.

TRADING LOGBOOK ⇄

Rules No.

Rules No.

Rules No.

Rules No.

TRADING LOGBOOK

○ Mon ○ Tue ○ Wed ○ Thu ○ Fri ○ Sat ○ Sun 📅 Date : _____

Market Conditions	Available Funds

☐ Options   ☐ Stocks   ☐ Forex   ☐ Futures   ☐ Crypto

Time	Name	Quantity	Buy/Sell	Price	Cost	Profit/Loss	Balance

Target / Stop :	

TRADING LOGBOOK

○ Mon ○ Tue ○ Wed ○ Thu ○ Fri ○ Sat ○ Sun 📅 Date: _____

Market Conditions	Available Funds

☐ Options ☐ Stocks ☐ Forex ☐ Futures ☐ Crypto

Time	Name	Quantity	Buy/Sell	Price	Cost	Profit/Loss	Balance

Target / Stop :	

TRADING LOGBOOK

○ Mon ○ Tue ○ Wed ○ Thu ○ Fri ○ Sat ○ Sun 📅 Date : ....

Market Conditions	Available Funds

☐ Options ☐ Stocks ☐ Forex ☐ Futures ☐ Crypto

Time	Name	Quantity	Buy/Sell	Price	Cost	Profit/Loss	Balance

Target / Stop :	

TRADING LOGBOOK

○ Mon ○ Tue ○ Wed ○ Thu ○ Fri ○ Sat ○ Sun 📅 Date : _____

Market Conditions	Available Funds

☐ Options ☐ Stocks ☐ Forex ☐ Futures ☐ Crypto

Time	Name	Quantity	Buy/Sell	Price	Cost	Profit/Loss	Balance

Target / Stop :	

TRADING LOGBOOK

○ Mon ○ Tue ○ Wed ○ Thu ○ Fri ○ Sat ○ Sun 📅 Date : _____

Market Conditions	Available Funds

□ Options   □ Stocks   □ Forex   □ Futures   □ Crypto

Time	Name	Quantity	Buy/Sell	Price	Cost	Profit/Loss	Balance

Target / Stop :	

TRADING LOGBOOK

○ Mon ○ Tue ○ Wed ○ Thu ○ Fri ○ Sat ○ Sun 📅 Date: ....

Market Conditions	Available Funds

☐ Options ☐ Stocks ☐ Forex ☐ Futures ☐ Crypto

Time	Name	Quantity	Buy/Sell	Price	Cost	Profit/Loss	Balance

Target / Stop :	

TRADING LOGBOOK

○ Mon ○ Tue ○ Wed ○ Thu ○ Fri ○ Sat ○ Sun 📅 Date : ....

Market Conditions	Available Funds

☐ Options   ☐ Stocks   ☐ Forex   ☐ Futures   ☐ Crypto

Time	Name	Quantity	Buy/Sell	Price	Cost	Profit/Loss	Balance

Target / Stop :	

TRADING LOGBOOK

○ Mon ○ Tue ○ Wed ○ Thu ○ Fri ○ Sat ○ Sun 📅 Date : _____

Market Conditions	Available Funds

☐ Options   ☐ Stocks   ☐ Forex   ☐ Futures   ☐ Crypto

Time	Name	Quantity	Buy/Sell	Price	Cost	Profit/Loss	Balance

Target / Stop :	

TRADING LOGBOOK

○ Mon ○ Tue ○ Wed ○ Thu ○ Fri ○ Sat ○ Sun 📅 Date : _____

Market Conditions	Available Funds

☐ Options   ☐ Stocks   ☐ Forex   ☐ Futures   ☐ Crypto

Time	Name	Quantity	Buy/Sell	Price	Cost	Profit/Loss	Balance

Target / Stop :	

TRADING LOGBOOK

○ Mon ○ Tue ○ Wed ○ Thu ○ Fri ○ Sat ○ Sun 📅 Date : _____

Market Conditions	Available Funds

☐ Options   ☐ Stocks   ☐ Forex   ☐ Futures   ☐ Crypto

Time	Name	Quantity	Buy/Sell	Price	Cost	Profit/Loss	Balance

Target / Stop :	

TRADING LOGBOOK

○ Mon ○ Tue ○ Wed ○ Thu ○ Fri ○ Sat ○ Sun 📅 Date : ....

Market Conditions	Available Funds

☐ Options   ☐ Stocks   ☐ Forex   ☐ Futures   ☐ Crypto

Time	Name	Quantity	Buy/Sell	Price	Cost	Profit/Loss	Balance

Target / Stop :	

TRADING LOGBOOK

○ Mon ○ Tue ○ Wed ○ Thu ○ Fri ○ Sat ○ Sun 📅 Date : _____

Market Conditions	Available Funds

☐ Options   ☐ Stocks   ☐ Forex   ☐ Futures   ☐ Crypto

Time	Name	Quantity	Buy/Sell	Price	Cost	Profit/Loss	Balance

Target / Stop :	

TRADING LOGBOOK

○ Mon ○ Tue ○ Wed ○ Thu ○ Fri ○ Sat ○ Sun 🗓 Date : _____

Market Conditions	Available Funds

☐ Options ☐ Stocks ☐ Forex ☐ Futures ☐ Crypto

Time	Name	Quantity	Buy/Sell	Price	Cost	Profit/Loss	Balance

Target / Stop :	

TRADING LOGBOOK

○ Mon ○ Tue ○ Wed ○ Thu ○ Fri ○ Sat ○ Sun 📆 Date: _____

Market Conditions	Available Funds

☐ Options   ☐ Stocks   ☐ Forex   ☐ Futures   ☐ Crypto

Time	Name	Quantity	Buy/Sell	Price	Cost	Profit/Loss	Balance

Target / Stop :	

TRADING LOGBOOK

○ Mon ○ Tue ○ Wed ○ Thu ○ Fri ○ Sat ○ Sun 📅 Date :

Market Conditions	Available Funds

☐ Options　☐ Stocks　☐ Forex　☐ Futures　☐ Crypto

Time	Name	Quantity	Buy/Sell	Price	Cost	Profit/Loss	Balance

Target / Stop :	

TRADING LOGBOOK

○ Mon ○ Tue ○ Wed ○ Thu ○ Fri ○ Sat ○ Sun 📅 Date : _____

Market Conditions	Available Funds

☐ Options ☐ Stocks ☐ Forex ☐ Futures ☐ Crypto

Time	Name	Quantity	Buy/Sell	Price	Cost	Profit/Loss	Balance

Target / Stop :	

TRADING LOGBOOK

○ Mon ○ Tue ○ Wed ○ Thu ○ Fri ○ Sat ○ Sun 📅 Date : ....

Market Conditions	Available Funds

☐ Options ☐ Stocks ☐ Forex ☐ Futures ☐ Crypto

Time	Name	Quantity	Buy/Sell	Price	Cost	Profit/Loss	Balance

Target / Stop :	

TRADING LOGBOOK

○ Mon ○ Tue ○ Wed ○ Thu ○ Fri ○ Sat ○ Sun 📅 Date: _____

Market Conditions	Available Funds

☐ Options ☐ Stocks ☐ Forex ☐ Futures ☐ Crypto

Time	Name	Quantity	Buy/Sell	Price	Cost	Profit/Loss	Balance

Target / Stop :	

TRADING LOGBOOK

○ Mon ○ Tue ○ Wed ○ Thu ○ Fri ○ Sat ○ Sun 📅 Date : ....

Market Conditions	Available Funds

☐ Options ☐ Stocks ☐ Forex ☐ Futures ☐ Crypto

Time	Name	Quantity	Buy/Sell	Price	Cost	Profit/Loss	Balance

Target / Stop :	

TRADING LOGBOOK

○ Mon ○ Tue ○ Wed ○ Thu ○ Fri ○ Sat ○ Sun 📅 Date: _____

Market Conditions	Available Funds

☐ Options   ☐ Stocks   ☐ Forex   ☐ Futures   ☐ Crypto

Time	Name	Quantity	Buy/Sell	Price	Cost	Profit/Loss	Balance

Target / Stop :	

TRADING LOGBOOK

○ Mon ○ Tue ○ Wed ○ Thu ○ Fri ○ Sat ○ Sun 📅 Date : _____

Market Conditions	Available Funds

☐ Options ☐ Stocks ☐ Forex ☐ Futures ☐ Crypto

Time	Name	Quantity	Buy/Sell	Price	Cost	Profit/Loss	Balance

Target / Stop :	

TRADING LOGBOOK

○ Mon ○ Tue ○ Wed ○ Thu ○ Fri ○ Sat ○ Sun 📅 Date : _____

Market Conditions	Available Funds

☐ Options   ☐ Stocks   ☐ Forex   ☐ Futures   ☐ Crypto

Time	Name	Quantity	Buy/Sell	Price	Cost	Profit/Loss	Balance

Target / Stop :	

TRADING LOGBOOK

○ Mon ○ Tue ○ Wed ○ Thu ○ Fri ○ Sat ○ Sun 📅 Date :

Market Conditions	Available Funds

☐ Options ☐ Stocks ☐ Forex ☐ Futures ☐ Crypto

Time	Name	Quantity	Buy/Sell	Price	Cost	Profit/Loss	Balance

Target / Stop :	

TRADING LOGBOOK

○ Mon ○ Tue ○ Wed ○ Thu ○ Fri ○ Sat ○ Sun 📅 Date: _____

Market Conditions	Available Funds

☐ Options ☐ Stocks ☐ Forex ☐ Futures ☐ Crypto

Time	Name	Quantity	Buy/Sell	Price	Cost	Profit/Loss	Balance

Target / Stop :	

TRADING LOGBOOK

○ Mon ○ Tue ○ Wed ○ Thu ○ Fri ○ Sat ○ Sun 📅 Date : _____

Market Conditions	Available Funds

☐ Options   ☐ Stocks   ☐ Forex   ☐ Futures   ☐ Crypto

Time	Name	Quantity	Buy/Sell	Price	Cost	Profit/Loss	Balance

Target / Stop :	

TRADING LOGBOOK

○ Mon ○ Tue ○ Wed ○ Thu ○ Fri ○ Sat ○ Sun 📅 Date : _____

Market Conditions	Available Funds

☐ Options   ☐ Stocks   ☐ Forex   ☐ Futures   ☐ Crypto

Time	Name	Quantity	Buy/Sell	Price	Cost	Profit/Loss	Balance

Target / Stop :	

TRADING LOGBOOK

○ Mon ○ Tue ○ Wed ○ Thu ○ Fri ○ Sat ○ Sun 📅 Date : ....

Market Conditions	Available Funds

☐ Options   ☐ Stocks   ☐ Forex   ☐ Futures   ☐ Crypto

Time	Name	Quantity	Buy/Sell	Price	Cost	Profit/Loss	Balance

Target / Stop :	

TRADING LOGBOOK

○ Mon ○ Tue ○ Wed ○ Thu ○ Fri ○ Sat ○ Sun 🗓 Date: _____

Market Conditions	Available Funds

☐ Options ☐ Stocks ☐ Forex ☐ Futures ☐ Crypto

Time	Name	Quantity	Buy/Sell	Price	Cost	Profit/Loss	Balance

Target / Stop :	

TRADING LOGBOOK

○ Mon ○ Tue ○ Wed ○ Thu ○ Fri ○ Sat ○ Sun 📅 Date : _____

Market Conditions	Available Funds

☐ Options   ☐ Stocks   ☐ Forex   ☐ Futures   ☐ Crypto

Time	Name	Quantity	Buy/Sell	Price	Cost	Profit/Loss	Balance

Target / Stop :	

TRADING LOGBOOK

○ Mon ○ Tue ○ Wed ○ Thu ○ Fri ○ Sat ○ Sun 📅 Date : _____

Market Conditions	Available Funds

☐ Options ☐ Stocks ☐ Forex ☐ Futures ☐ Crypto

Time	Name	Quantity	Buy/Sell	Price	Cost	Profit/Loss	Balance

Target / Stop :	

TRADING LOGBOOK

○ Mon ○ Tue ○ Wed ○ Thu ○ Fri ○ Sat ○ Sun 📅 Date : _____

Market Conditions	Available Funds

☐ Options   ☐ Stocks   ☐ Forex   ☐ Futures   ☐ Crypto

Time	Name	Quantity	Buy/Sell	Price	Cost	Profit/Loss	Balance

Target / Stop :	

TRADING LOGBOOK

○ Mon ○ Tue ○ Wed ○ Thu ○ Fri ○ Sat ○ Sun 📅 Date : _____

Market Conditions	Available Funds

☐ Options   ☐ Stocks   ☐ Forex   ☐ Futures   ☐ Crypto

Time	Name	Quantity	Buy/Sell	Price	Cost	Profit/Loss	Balance

Target / Stop :	

TRADING LOGBOOK

○ Mon ○ Tue ○ Wed ○ Thu ○ Fri ○ Sat ○ Sun 📅 Date : ....

Market Conditions	Available Funds

☐ Options ☐ Stocks ☐ Forex ☐ Futures ☐ Crypto

Time	Name	Quantity	Buy/Sell	Price	Cost	Profit/Loss	Balance

Target / Stop :	

TRADING LOGBOOK

○ Mon ○ Tue ○ Wed ○ Thu ○ Fri ○ Sat ○ Sun 🗓 Date: _____

Market Conditions	Available Funds

☐ Options　☐ Stocks　☐ Forex　☐ Futures　☐ Crypto

Time	Name	Quantity	Buy/Sell	Price	Cost	Profit/Loss	Balance

Target / Stop :	

TRADING LOGBOOK

○ Mon ○ Tue ○ Wed ○ Thu ○ Fri ○ Sat ○ Sun 🗓 Date : ....

Market Conditions	Available Funds

□ Options □ Stocks □ Forex □ Futures □ Crypto

Time	Name	Quantity	Buy/Sell	Price	Cost	Profit/Loss	Balance

Target / Stop :	

TRADING LOGBOOK

○ Mon ○ Tue ○ Wed ○ Thu ○ Fri ○ Sat ○ Sun 📅 Date : _____

Market Conditions	Available Funds

☐ Options ☐ Stocks ☐ Forex ☐ Futures ☐ Crypto

Time	Name	Quantity	Buy/Sell	Price	Cost	Profit/Loss	Balance

Target / Stop :	

TRADING LOGBOOK

○ Mon ○ Tue ○ Wed ○ Thu ○ Fri ○ Sat ○ Sun 📅 Date : _____

Market Conditions	Available Funds

□ Options □ Stocks □ Forex □ Futures □ Crypto

Time	Name	Quantity	Buy/Sell	Price	Cost	Profit/Loss	Balance

Target / Stop :	

TRADING LOGBOOK

○ Mon ○ Tue ○ Wed ○ Thu ○ Fri ○ Sat ○ Sun 🗓 Date : _____

Market Conditions	Available Funds

☐ Options   ☐ Stocks   ☐ Forex   ☐ Futures   ☐ Crypto

Time	Name	Quantity	Buy/Sell	Price	Cost	Profit/Loss	Balance

Target / Stop :	

TRADING LOGBOOK

○ Mon ○ Tue ○ Wed ○ Thu ○ Fri ○ Sat ○ Sun 📅 Date : _____

Market Conditions	Available Funds

☐ Options ☐ Stocks ☐ Forex ☐ Futures ☐ Crypto

Time	Name	Quantity	Buy/Sell	Price	Cost	Profit/Loss	Balance

Target / Stop :	

TRADING LOGBOOK

○ Mon ○ Tue ○ Wed ○ Thu ○ Fri ○ Sat ○ Sun 📅 Date: ....

Market Conditions	Available Funds

☐ Options ☐ Stocks ☐ Forex ☐ Futures ☐ Crypto

Time	Name	Quantity	Buy/Sell	Price	Cost	Profit/Loss	Balance

Target / Stop :	

TRADING LOGBOOK

○ Mon ○ Tue ○ Wed ○ Thu ○ Fri ○ Sat ○ Sun 📅 Date : ....

Market Conditions	Available Funds

☐ Options   ☐ Stocks   ☐ Forex   ☐ Futures   ☐ Crypto

Time	Name	Quantity	Buy/Sell	Price	Cost	Profit/Loss	Balance

Target / Stop :	

TRADING LOGBOOK

○ Mon ○ Tue ○ Wed ○ Thu ○ Fri ○ Sat ○ Sun 📅 Date: _____

Market Conditions	Available Funds

☐ Options   ☐ Stocks   ☐ Forex   ☐ Futures   ☐ Crypto

Time	Name	Quantity	Buy/Sell	Price	Cost	Profit/Loss	Balance

Target / Stop :	

TRADING LOGBOOK

○ Mon ○ Tue ○ Wed ○ Thu ○ Fri ○ Sat ○ Sun 📅 Date :

Market Conditions	Available Funds

☐ Options ☐ Stocks ☐ Forex ☐ Futures ☐ Crypto

Time	Name	Quantity	Buy/Sell	Price	Cost	Profit/Loss	Balance

Target / Stop :	

TRADING LOGBOOK

○ Mon ○ Tue ○ Wed ○ Thu ○ Fri ○ Sat ○ Sun 📅 Date : _____

Market Conditions	Available Funds

☐ Options ☐ Stocks ☐ Forex ☐ Futures ☐ Crypto

Time	Name	Quantity	Buy/Sell	Price	Cost	Profit/Loss	Balance

Target / Stop :	

TRADING LOGBOOK

○ Mon ○ Tue ○ Wed ○ Thu ○ Fri ○ Sat ○ Sun 📅 Date : ....

Market Conditions	Available Funds

☐ Options ☐ Stocks ☐ Forex ☐ Futures ☐ Crypto

Time	Name	Quantity	Buy/Sell	Price	Cost	Profit/Loss	Balance

Target / Stop :	

TRADING LOGBOOK

○ Mon ○ Tue ○ Wed ○ Thu ○ Fri ○ Sat ○ Sun 📅 Date : _____

Market Conditions	Available Funds

☐ Options ☐ Stocks ☐ Forex ☐ Futures ☐ Crypto

Time	Name	Quantity	Buy/Sell	Price	Cost	Profit/Loss	Balance

Target / Stop :	

TRADING LOGBOOK

○ Mon ○ Tue ○ Wed ○ Thu ○ Fri ○ Sat ○ Sun 📅 Date : ....

Market Conditions	Available Funds

☐ Options   ☐ Stocks   ☐ Forex   ☐ Futures   ☐ Crypto

Time	Name	Quantity	Buy/Sell	Price	Cost	Profit/Loss	Balance

Target / Stop :	

TRADING LOGBOOK

○ Mon ○ Tue ○ Wed ○ Thu ○ Fri ○ Sat ○ Sun 🗓 Date: ....

Market Conditions	Available Funds

☐ Options ☐ Stocks ☐ Forex ☐ Futures ☐ Crypto

Time	Name	Quantity	Buy/Sell	Price	Cost	Profit/Loss	Balance

Target / Stop :	

TRADING LOGBOOK

○ Mon ○ Tue ○ Wed ○ Thu ○ Fri ○ Sat ○ Sun 📅 Date : _____

Market Conditions	Available Funds

☐ Options ☐ Stocks ☐ Forex ☐ Futures ☐ Crypto

Time	Name	Quantity	Buy/Sell	Price	Cost	Profit/Loss	Balance

Target / Stop :	

TRADING LOGBOOK

○ Mon ○ Tue ○ Wed ○ Thu ○ Fri ○ Sat ○ Sun 📅 Date : _____

Market Conditions	Available Funds

☐ Options   ☐ Stocks   ☐ Forex   ☐ Futures   ☐ Crypto

Time	Name	Quantity	Buy/Sell	Price	Cost	Profit/Loss	Balance

Target / Stop :	

TRADING LOGBOOK

○ Mon ○ Tue ○ Wed ○ Thu ○ Fri ○ Sat ○ Sun 🗓 Date :

Market Conditions	Available Funds

□ Options   □ Stocks   □ Forex   □ Futures   □ Crypto

Time	Name	Quantity	Buy/Sell	Price	Cost	Profit/Loss	Balance

Target / Stop :	

TRADING LOGBOOK

○ Mon ○ Tue ○ Wed ○ Thu ○ Fri ○ Sat ○ Sun 🗓 Date : _____

Market Conditions	Available Funds

☐ Options ☐ Stocks ☐ Forex ☐ Futures ☐ Crypto

Time	Name	Quantity	Buy/Sell	Price	Cost	Profit/Loss	Balance

Target / Stop :	

TRADING LOGBOOK

○ Mon ○ Tue ○ Wed ○ Thu ○ Fri ○ Sat ○ Sun 📅 Date : ....

Market Conditions	Available Funds

☐ Options ☐ Stocks ☐ Forex ☐ Futures ☐ Crypto

Time	Name	Quantity	Buy/Sell	Price	Cost	Profit/Loss	Balance

Target / Stop :	

TRADING LOGBOOK

○ Mon ○ Tue ○ Wed ○ Thu ○ Fri ○ Sat ○ Sun 📅 Date: _____

Market Conditions	Available Funds

☐ Options ☐ Stocks ☐ Forex ☐ Futures ☐ Crypto

Time	Name	Quantity	Buy/Sell	Price	Cost	Profit/Loss	Balance

Target / Stop :	

TRADING LOGBOOK

○ Mon ○ Tue ○ Wed ○ Thu ○ Fri ○ Sat ○ Sun 📅 Date : ....

Market Conditions	Available Funds

☐ Options ☐ Stocks ☐ Forex ☐ Futures ☐ Crypto

Time	Name	Quantity	Buy/Sell	Price	Cost	Profit/Loss	Balance

Target / Stop :	

TRADING LOGBOOK

○ Mon ○ Tue ○ Wed ○ Thu ○ Fri ○ Sat ○ Sun 📅 Date : _____

Market Conditions	Available Funds

☐ Options ☐ Stocks ☐ Forex ☐ Futures ☐ Crypto

Time	Name	Quantity	Buy/Sell	Price	Cost	Profit/Loss	Balance

Target / Stop :	

TRADING LOGBOOK

○ Mon ○ Tue ○ Wed ○ Thu ○ Fri ○ Sat ○ Sun 📅 Date :

Market Conditions	Available Funds

☐ Options ☐ Stocks ☐ Forex ☐ Futures ☐ Crypto

Time	Name	Quantity	Buy/Sell	Price	Cost	Profit/Loss	Balance

Target / Stop :	

TRADING LOGBOOK

○ Mon ○ Tue ○ Wed ○ Thu ○ Fri ○ Sat ○ Sun 🗓 Date : _____

Market Conditions	Available Funds

☐ Options   ☐ Stocks   ☐ Forex   ☐ Futures   ☐ Crypto

Time	Name	Quantity	Buy/Sell	Price	Cost	Profit/Loss	Balance

Target / Stop :	

TRADING LOGBOOK

○ Mon ○ Tue ○ Wed ○ Thu ○ Fri ○ Sat ○ Sun 📅 Date :

Market Conditions	Available Funds

☐ Options ☐ Stocks ☐ Forex ☐ Futures ☐ Crypto

Time	Name	Quantity	Buy/Sell	Price	Cost	Profit/Loss	Balance

Target / Stop :	

TRADING LOGBOOK

○ Mon ○ Tue ○ Wed ○ Thu ○ Fri ○ Sat ○ Sun   Date: _____

Market Conditions	Available Funds

☐ Options   ☐ Stocks   ☐ Forex   ☐ Futures   ☐ Crypto

Time	Name	Quantity	Buy/Sell	Price	Cost	Profit/Loss	Balance

Target / Stop :	

TRADING LOGBOOK

○ Mon ○ Tue ○ Wed ○ Thu ○ Fri ○ Sat ○ Sun 📅 Date : _____

Market Conditions	Available Funds

☐ Options ☐ Stocks ☐ Forex ☐ Futures ☐ Crypto

Time	Name	Quantity	Buy/Sell	Price	Cost	Profit/Loss	Balance

Target / Stop :	

TRADING LOGBOOK

○ Mon ○ Tue ○ Wed ○ Thu ○ Fri ○ Sat ○ Sun 📅 Date: ....

Market Conditions	Available Funds

☐ Options   ☐ Stocks   ☐ Forex   ☐ Futures   ☐ Crypto

Time	Name	Quantity	Buy/Sell	Price	Cost	Profit/Loss	Balance

Target / Stop :	

TRADING LOGBOOK

○ Mon ○ Tue ○ Wed ○ Thu ○ Fri ○ Sat ○ Sun 📅 Date : _____

Market Conditions	Available Funds

☐ Options   ☐ Stocks   ☐ Forex   ☐ Futures   ☐ Crypto

Time	Name	Quantity	Buy/Sell	Price	Cost	Profit/Loss	Balance

Target / Stop :	

TRADING LOGBOOK

○ Mon ○ Tue ○ Wed ○ Thu ○ Fri ○ Sat ○ Sun 🗓 Date: _____

Market Conditions	Available Funds

☐ Options ☐ Stocks ☐ Forex ☐ Futures ☐ Crypto

Time	Name	Quantity	Buy/Sell	Price	Cost	Profit/Loss	Balance

Target / Stop :	

TRADING LOGBOOK

○ Mon ○ Tue ○ Wed ○ Thu ○ Fri ○ Sat ○ Sun 📅 Date : _____

Market Conditions	Available Funds

☐ Options   ☐ Stocks   ☐ Forex   ☐ Futures   ☐ Crypto

Time	Name	Quantity	Buy/Sell	Price	Cost	Profit/Loss	Balance

Target / Stop :	

TRADING LOGBOOK

○ Mon ○ Tue ○ Wed ○ Thu ○ Fri ○ Sat ○ Sun 📅 Date : _____

Market Conditions	Available Funds

□ Options   □ Stocks   □ Forex   □ Futures   □ Crypto

Time	Name	Quantity	Buy/Sell	Price	Cost	Profit/Loss	Balance

Target / Stop :	

TRADING LOGBOOK

○ Mon ○ Tue ○ Wed ○ Thu ○ Fri ○ Sat ○ Sun 📅 Date : ....

Market Conditions	Available Funds

☐ Options ☐ Stocks ☐ Forex ☐ Futures ☐ Crypto

Time	Name	Quantity	Buy/Sell	Price	Cost	Profit/Loss	Balance

Target / Stop :	

TRADING LOGBOOK

○ Mon ○ Tue ○ Wed ○ Thu ○ Fri ○ Sat ○ Sun 📅 Date : _____

Market Conditions	Available Funds

☐ Options ☐ Stocks ☐ Forex ☐ Futures ☐ Crypto

Time	Name	Quantity	Buy/Sell	Price	Cost	Profit/Loss	Balance

Target / Stop :	

TRADING LOGBOOK

○ Mon ○ Tue ○ Wed ○ Thu ○ Fri ○ Sat ○ Sun 📅 Date : _____

Market Conditions	Available Funds

☐ Options ☐ Stocks ☐ Forex ☐ Futures ☐ Crypto

Time	Name	Quantity	Buy/Sell	Price	Cost	Profit/Loss	Balance

Target / Stop :	

TRADING LOGBOOK

○ Mon ○ Tue ○ Wed ○ Thu ○ Fri ○ Sat ○ Sun 📅 Date : _____

Market Conditions	Available Funds

☐ Options ☐ Stocks ☐ Forex ☐ Futures ☐ Crypto

Time	Name	Quantity	Buy/Sell	Price	Cost	Profit/Loss	Balance

Target / Stop :	

TRADING LOGBOOK

○ Mon ○ Tue ○ Wed ○ Thu ○ Fri ○ Sat ○ Sun 🗓 Date : ....

Market Conditions	Available Funds

☐ Options   ☐ Stocks   ☐ Forex   ☐ Futures   ☐ Crypto

Time	Name	Quantity	Buy/Sell	Price	Cost	Profit/Loss	Balance

Target / Stop :	

TRADING LOGBOOK

Market Conditions	Available Funds

☐ Options ☐ Stocks ☐ Forex ☐ Futures ☐ Crypto

Time	Name	Quantity	Buy/Sell	Price	Cost	Profit/Loss	Balance

Target / Stop :	

TRADING LOGBOOK

○ Mon ○ Tue ○ Wed ○ Thu ○ Fri ○ Sat ○ Sun 📅 Date : ....

Market Conditions	Available Funds

☐ Options   ☐ Stocks   ☐ Forex   ☐ Futures   ☐ Crypto

Time	Name	Quantity	Buy/Sell	Price	Cost	Profit/Loss	Balance

Target / Stop :	

TRADING LOGBOOK

○ Mon ○ Tue ○ Wed ○ Thu ○ Fri ○ Sat ○ Sun 📅 Date : _____

Market Conditions	Available Funds

☐ Options ☐ Stocks ☐ Forex ☐ Futures ☐ Crypto

Time	Name	Quantity	Buy/Sell	Price	Cost	Profit/Loss	Balance

Target / Stop :	

TRADING LOGBOOK

○ Mon ○ Tue ○ Wed ○ Thu ○ Fri ○ Sat ○ Sun 📆 Date : ....

Market Conditions	Available Funds

☐ Options   ☐ Stocks   ☐ Forex   ☐ Futures   ☐ Crypto

Time	Name	Quantity	Buy/Sell	Price	Cost	Profit/Loss	Balance

Target / Stop :	

TRADING LOGBOOK

○ Mon ○ Tue ○ Wed ○ Thu ○ Fri ○ Sat ○ Sun   🗓 Date : ....

Market Conditions	Available Funds

☐ Options   ☐ Stocks   ☐ Forex   ☐ Futures   ☐ Crypto

Time	Name	Quantity	Buy/Sell	Price	Cost	Profit/Loss	Balance

Target / Stop :	

TRADING LOGBOOK

○ Mon ○ Tue ○ Wed ○ Thu ○ Fri ○ Sat ○ Sun 📅 Date : _____

Market Conditions	Available Funds

☐ Options ☐ Stocks ☐ Forex ☐ Futures ☐ Crypto

Time	Name	Quantity	Buy/Sell	Price	Cost	Profit/Loss	Balance

Target / Stop :	

TRADING LOGBOOK

○ Mon ○ Tue ○ Wed ○ Thu ○ Fri ○ Sat ○ Sun 🗓 Date : _____

Market Conditions	Available Funds

☐ Options ☐ Stocks ☐ Forex ☐ Futures ☐ Crypto

Time	Name	Quantity	Buy/Sell	Price	Cost	Profit/Loss	Balance

Target / Stop :	

TRADING LOGBOOK

○ Mon ○ Tue ○ Wed ○ Thu ○ Fri ○ Sat ○ Sun 📅 Date : _____

Market Conditions	Available Funds

☐ Options ☐ Stocks ☐ Forex ☐ Futures ☐ Crypto

Time	Name	Quantity	Buy/Sell	Price	Cost	Profit/Loss	Balance

Target / Stop :	

TRADING LOGBOOK

○ Mon ○ Tue ○ Wed ○ Thu ○ Fri ○ Sat ○ Sun 🗓 Date : _____

Market Conditions	Available Funds

☐ Options ☐ Stocks ☐ Forex ☐ Futures ☐ Crypto

Time	Name	Quantity	Buy/Sell	Price	Cost	Profit/Loss	Balance

Target / Stop :	

TRADING LOGBOOK

○ Mon ○ Tue ○ Wed ○ Thu ○ Fri ○ Sat ○ Sun 📅 Date : ....

Market Conditions	Available Funds

☐ Options ☐ Stocks ☐ Forex ☐ Futures ☐ Crypto

Time	Name	Quantity	Buy/Sell	Price	Cost	Profit/Loss	Balance

Target / Stop :	

TRADING LOGBOOK

○ Mon ○ Tue ○ Wed ○ Thu ○ Fri ○ Sat ○ Sun 📅 Date : ....

Market Conditions	Available Funds

☐ Options ☐ Stocks ☐ Forex ☐ Futures ☐ Crypto

Time	Name	Quantity	Buy/Sell	Price	Cost	Profit/Loss	Balance

Target / Stop :	

TRADING LOGBOOK

○ Mon ○ Tue ○ Wed ○ Thu ○ Fri ○ Sat ○ Sun 🗓 Date : ....

Market Conditions	Available Funds

☐ Options   ☐ Stocks   ☐ Forex   ☐ Futures   ☐ Crypto

Time	Name	Quantity	Buy/Sell	Price	Cost	Profit/Loss	Balance

Target / Stop :	

TRADING LOGBOOK

○ Mon ○ Tue ○ Wed ○ Thu ○ Fri ○ Sat ○ Sun 🗓 Date : _____

Market Conditions	Available Funds

☐ Options ☐ Stocks ☐ Forex ☐ Futures ☐ Crypto

Time	Name	Quantity	Buy/Sell	Price	Cost	Profit/Loss	Balance

Target / Stop :	

TRADING LOGBOOK

○ Mon ○ Tue ○ Wed ○ Thu ○ Fri ○ Sat ○ Sun 📅 Date : _____

Market Conditions	Available Funds

☐ Options ☐ Stocks ☐ Forex ☐ Futures ☐ Crypto

Time	Name	Quantity	Buy/Sell	Price	Cost	Profit/Loss	Balance

Target / Stop :	

TRADING LOGBOOK

○ Mon ○ Tue ○ Wed ○ Thu ○ Fri ○ Sat ○ Sun 📅 Date : _____

Market Conditions	Available Funds

☐ Options   ☐ Stocks   ☐ Forex   ☐ Futures   ☐ Crypto

Time	Name	Quantity	Buy/Sell	Price	Cost	Profit/Loss	Balance

Target / Stop :	

TRADING LOGBOOK

○ Mon ○ Tue ○ Wed ○ Thu ○ Fri ○ Sat ○ Sun   📅 Date : ....

Market Conditions	Available Funds

☐ Options ☐ Stocks ☐ Forex ☐ Futures ☐ Crypto

Time	Name	Quantity	Buy/Sell	Price	Cost	Profit/Loss	Balance

Target / Stop :	

TRADING LOGBOOK

○ Mon ○ Tue ○ Wed ○ Thu ○ Fri ○ Sat ○ Sun 📅 Date: _____

Market Conditions	Available Funds

☐ Options ☐ Stocks ☐ Forex ☐ Futures ☐ Crypto

Time	Name	Quantity	Buy/Sell	Price	Cost	Profit/Loss	Balance

Target / Stop :	

TRADING LOGBOOK

○ Mon ○ Tue ○ Wed ○ Thu ○ Fri ○ Sat ○ Sun 🗓 Date : _____

Market Conditions	Available Funds

☐ Options   ☐ Stocks   ☐ Forex   ☐ Futures   ☐ Crypto

Time	Name	Quantity	Buy/Sell	Price	Cost	Profit/Loss	Balance

Target / Stop :	

TRADING LOGBOOK

○ Mon ○ Tue ○ Wed ○ Thu ○ Fri ○ Sat ○ Sun 📅 Date : ....

Market Conditions	Available Funds

☐ Options ☐ Stocks ☐ Forex ☐ Futures ☐ Crypto

Time	Name	Quantity	Buy/Sell	Price	Cost	Profit/Loss	Balance

Target / Stop :	

TRADING LOGBOOK

○ Mon ○ Tue ○ Wed ○ Thu ○ Fri ○ Sat ○ Sun 📅 Date : _____

Market Conditions	Available Funds

☐ Options ☐ Stocks ☐ Forex ☐ Futures ☐ Crypto

Time	Name	Quantity	Buy/Sell	Price	Cost	Profit/Loss	Balance

Target / Stop :	

TRADING LOGBOOK

○ Mon ○ Tue ○ Wed ○ Thu ○ Fri ○ Sat ○ Sun ▦ Date : _____

Market Conditions	Available Funds

☐ Options ☐ Stocks ☐ Forex ☐ Futures ☐ Crypto

Time	Name	Quantity	Buy/Sell	Price	Cost	Profit/Loss	Balance

Target / Stop :	

TRADING LOGBOOK

○ Mon ○ Tue ○ Wed ○ Thu ○ Fri ○ Sat ○ Sun 📅 Date : ....

Market Conditions	Available Funds

☐ Options   ☐ Stocks   ☐ Forex   ☐ Futures   ☐ Crypto

Time	Name	Quantity	Buy/Sell	Price	Cost	Profit/Loss	Balance

Target / Stop :	

TRADING LOGBOOK

○ Mon ○ Tue ○ Wed ○ Thu ○ Fri ○ Sat ○ Sun 🗓 Date : ....

Market Conditions	Available Funds

☐ Options   ☐ Stocks   ☐ Forex   ☐ Futures   ☐ Crypto

Time	Name	Quantity	Buy/Sell	Price	Cost	Profit/Loss	Balance

Target / Stop :	

TRADING LOGBOOK

○ Mon ○ Tue ○ Wed ○ Thu ○ Fri ○ Sat ○ Sun 📅 Date : ....

Market Conditions	Available Funds

☐ Options ☐ Stocks ☐ Forex ☐ Futures ☐ Crypto

Time	Name	Quantity	Buy/Sell	Price	Cost	Profit/Loss	Balance

Target / Stop :	

TRADING LOGBOOK

○ Mon ○ Tue ○ Wed ○ Thu ○ Fri ○ Sat ○ Sun 📅 Date : ....

Market Conditions	Available Funds

☐ Options   ☐ Stocks   ☐ Forex   ☐ Futures   ☐ Crypto

Time	Name	Quantity	Buy/Sell	Price	Cost	Profit/Loss	Balance

Target / Stop :	

TRADING LOGBOOK

○ Mon ○ Tue ○ Wed ○ Thu ○ Fri ○ Sat ○ Sun 📅 Date : _____

Market Conditions	Available Funds

☐ Options   ☐ Stocks   ☐ Forex   ☐ Futures   ☐ Crypto

Time	Name	Quantity	Buy/Sell	Price	Cost	Profit/Loss	Balance

Target / Stop :	

TRADING LOGBOOK

○ Mon ○ Tue ○ Wed ○ Thu ○ Fri ○ Sat ○ Sun 📅 Date : ....

Market Conditions	Available Funds

☐ Options ☐ Stocks ☐ Forex ☐ Futures ☐ Crypto

Time	Name	Quantity	Buy/Sell	Price	Cost	Profit/Loss	Balance

Target / Stop :	

TRADING LOGBOOK

○ Mon ○ Tue ○ Wed ○ Thu ○ Fri ○ Sat ○ Sun 📅 Date : _____

Market Conditions	Available Funds

□ Options □ Stocks □ Forex □ Futures □ Crypto

Time	Name	Quantity	Buy/Sell	Price	Cost	Profit/Loss	Balance

Target / Stop :	

TRADING LOGBOOK

○ Mon ○ Tue ○ Wed ○ Thu ○ Fri ○ Sat ○ Sun 📆 Date : ....

Market Conditions	Available Funds

☐ Options ☐ Stocks ☐ Forex ☐ Futures ☐ Crypto

Time	Name	Quantity	Buy/Sell	Price	Cost	Profit/Loss	Balance

Target / Stop :	

TRADING LOGBOOK

○ Mon ○ Tue ○ Wed ○ Thu ○ Fri ○ Sat ○ Sun 📅 Date : _____

Market Conditions	Available Funds

☐ Options ☐ Stocks ☐ Forex ☐ Futures ☐ Crypto

Time	Name	Quantity	Buy/Sell	Price	Cost	Profit/Loss	Balance

Target / Stop :	

TRADING LOGBOOK

○ Mon ○ Tue ○ Wed ○ Thu ○ Fri ○ Sat ○ Sun 📅 Date : _____

Market Conditions	Available Funds

☐ Options ☐ Stocks ☐ Forex ☐ Futures ☐ Crypto

Time	Name	Quantity	Buy/Sell	Price	Cost	Profit/Loss	Balance

Target / Stop :	

TRADING LOGBOOK

○ Mon ○ Tue ○ Wed ○ Thu ○ Fri ○ Sat ○ Sun 📅 Date : ....

Market Conditions	Available Funds

□ Options   □ Stocks   □ Forex   □ Futures   □ Crypto

Time	Name	Quantity	Buy/Sell	Price	Cost	Profit/Loss	Balance

Target / Stop :	

TRADING LOGBOOK

○ Mon ○ Tue ○ Wed ○ Thu ○ Fri ○ Sat ○ Sun 📅 Date : ....

Market Conditions	Available Funds

☐ Options ☐ Stocks ☐ Forex ☐ Futures ☐ Crypto

Time	Name	Quantity	Buy/Sell	Price	Cost	Profit/Loss	Balance

Target / Stop :	

TRADING LOGBOOK

○ Mon ○ Tue ○ Wed ○ Thu ○ Fri ○ Sat ○ Sun 🗓 Date : _____

Market Conditions	Available Funds

☐ Options   ☐ Stocks   ☐ Forex   ☐ Futures   ☐ Crypto

Time	Name	Quantity	Buy/Sell	Price	Cost	Profit/Loss	Balance

Target / Stop :	

TRADING LOGBOOK

○ Mon ○ Tue ○ Wed ○ Thu ○ Fri ○ Sat ○ Sun 📅 Date : ....

Market Conditions	Available Funds

☐ Options   ☐ Stocks   ☐ Forex   ☐ Futures   ☐ Crypto

Time	Name	Quantity	Buy/Sell	Price	Cost	Profit/Loss	Balance

Target / Stop :	

TRADING LOGBOOK

○ Mon ○ Tue ○ Wed ○ Thu ○ Fri ○ Sat ○ Sun 📅 Date : _____

Market Conditions	Available Funds

☐ Options ☐ Stocks ☐ Forex ☐ Futures ☐ Crypto

Time	Name	Quantity	Buy/Sell	Price	Cost	Profit/Loss	Balance

Target / Stop :	

TRADING LOGBOOK

○ Mon ○ Tue ○ Wed ○ Thu ○ Fri ○ Sat ○ Sun 📅 Date: _____

Market Conditions	Available Funds

☐ Options ☐ Stocks ☐ Forex ☐ Futures ☐ Crypto

Time	Name	Quantity	Buy/Sell	Price	Cost	Profit/Loss	Balance

Target / Stop :	

TRADING LOGBOOK

○ Mon ○ Tue ○ Wed ○ Thu ○ Fri ○ Sat ○ Sun 📅 Date : ....

Market Conditions	Available Funds

☐ Options ☐ Stocks ☐ Forex ☐ Futures ☐ Crypto

Time	Name	Quantity	Buy/Sell	Price	Cost	Profit/Loss	Balance

Target / Stop :	

TRADING LOGBOOK

○ Mon ○ Tue ○ Wed ○ Thu ○ Fri ○ Sat ○ Sun 🗓 Date : _____

Market Conditions	Available Funds

☐ Options ☐ Stocks ☐ Forex ☐ Futures ☐ Crypto

Time	Name	Quantity	Buy/Sell	Price	Cost	Profit/Loss	Balance

Target / Stop :	

TRADING LOGBOOK

○ Mon ○ Tue ○ Wed ○ Thu ○ Fri ○ Sat ○ Sun 📅 Date : _____

Market Conditions	Available Funds

☐ Options ☐ Stocks ☐ Forex ☐ Futures ☐ Crypto

Time	Name	Quantity	Buy/Sell	Price	Cost	Profit/Loss	Balance

Target / Stop :	

TRADING LOGBOOK

○ Mon ○ Tue ○ Wed ○ Thu ○ Fri ○ Sat ○ Sun 📅 Date : ....

Market Conditions	Available Funds

☐ Options　☐ Stocks　☐ Forex　☐ Futures　☐ Crypto

Time	Name	Quantity	Buy/Sell	Price	Cost	Profit/Loss	Balance

Target / Stop :	

TRADING LOGBOOK

○ Mon ○ Tue ○ Wed ○ Thu ○ Fri ○ Sat ○ Sun 🗓 Date : ....

Market Conditions	Available Funds

☐ Options   ☐ Stocks   ☐ Forex   ☐ Futures   ☐ Crypto

Time	Name	Quantity	Buy/Sell	Price	Cost	Profit/Loss	Balance

Target / Stop :	

TRADING LOGBOOK

○ Mon ○ Tue ○ Wed ○ Thu ○ Fri ○ Sat ○ Sun 🗓 Date : _____

Market Conditions	Available Funds

☐ Options   ☐ Stocks   ☐ Forex   ☐ Futures   ☐ Crypto

Time	Name	Quantity	Buy/Sell	Price	Cost	Profit/Loss	Balance

Target / Stop :	

TRADING LOGBOOK

○ Mon ○ Tue ○ Wed ○ Thu ○ Fri ○ Sat ○ Sun 📅 Date : ....

Market Conditions	Available Funds

☐ Options ☐ Stocks ☐ Forex ☐ Futures ☐ Crypto

Time	Name	Quantity	Buy/Sell	Price	Cost	Profit/Loss	Balance

Target / Stop :	

TRADING LOGBOOK

○ Mon ○ Tue ○ Wed ○ Thu ○ Fri ○ Sat ○ Sun 📅 Date : _____

Market Conditions	Available Funds

□ Options   □ Stocks   □ Forex   □ Futures   □ Crypto

Time	Name	Quantity	Buy/Sell	Price	Cost	Profit/Loss	Balance

Target / Stop :	

TRADING LOGBOOK

○ Mon ○ Tue ○ Wed ○ Thu ○ Fri ○ Sat ○ Sun 📅 Date : _____

Market Conditions	Available Funds

☐ Options ☐ Stocks ☐ Forex ☐ Futures ☐ Crypto

Time	Name	Quantity	Buy/Sell	Price	Cost	Profit/Loss	Balance

Target / Stop :	

TRADING LOGBOOK

○ Mon ○ Tue ○ Wed ○ Thu ○ Fri ○ Sat ○ Sun 🗓 Date : ....

Market Conditions	Available Funds

☐ Options   ☐ Stocks   ☐ Forex   ☐ Futures   ☐ Crypto

Time	Name	Quantity	Buy/Sell	Price	Cost	Profit/Loss	Balance

Target / Stop :	

TRADING LOGBOOK

○ Mon ○ Tue ○ Wed ○ Thu ○ Fri ○ Sat ○ Sun 📅 Date : ....

Market Conditions	Available Funds

☐ Options   ☐ Stocks   ☐ Forex   ☐ Futures   ☐ Crypto

Time	Name	Quantity	Buy/Sell	Price	Cost	Profit/Loss	Balance

Target / Stop :	

TRADING LOGBOOK

Market Conditions	Available Funds

☐ Options   ☐ Stocks   ☐ Forex   ☐ Futures   ☐ Crypto

Time	Name	Quantity	Buy/Sell	Price	Cost	Profit/Loss	Balance

Target / Stop :	

TRADING LOGBOOK

○ Mon ○ Tue ○ Wed ○ Thu ○ Fri ○ Sat ○ Sun 📅 Date : _____

Market Conditions	Available Funds

□ Options   □ Stocks   □ Forex   □ Futures   □ Crypto

Time	Name	Quantity	Buy/Sell	Price	Cost	Profit/Loss	Balance

Target / Stop :	

TRADING LOGBOOK

○ Mon ○ Tue ○ Wed ○ Thu ○ Fri ○ Sat ○ Sun 📅 Date : _____

Market Conditions	Available Funds

☐ Options ☐ Stocks ☐ Forex ☐ Futures ☐ Crypto

Time	Name	Quantity	Buy/Sell	Price	Cost	Profit/Loss	Balance

Target / Stop :

TRADING LOGBOOK

○ Mon ○ Tue ○ Wed ○ Thu ○ Fri ○ Sat ○ Sun 🗓 Date : ....

Market Conditions	Available Funds

□ Options   □ Stocks   □ Forex   □ Futures   □ Crypto

Time	Name	Quantity	Buy/Sell	Price	Cost	Profit/Loss	Balance

Target / Stop :	

TRADING LOGBOOK

○ Mon ○ Tue ○ Wed ○ Thu ○ Fri ○ Sat ○ Sun 📅 Date : ....

Market Conditions	Available Funds

☐ Options ☐ Stocks ☐ Forex ☐ Futures ☐ Crypto

Time	Name	Quantity	Buy/Sell	Price	Cost	Profit/Loss	Balance

Target / Stop :	

TRADING LOGBOOK

○ Mon ○ Tue ○ Wed ○ Thu ○ Fri ○ Sat ○ Sun 📅 Date : ....

Market Conditions	Available Funds

☐ Options ☐ Stocks ☐ Forex ☐ Futures ☐ Crypto

Time	Name	Quantity	Buy/Sell	Price	Cost	Profit/Loss	Balance

Target / Stop :	

TRADING LOGBOOK

○ Mon ○ Tue ○ Wed ○ Thu ○ Fri ○ Sat ○ Sun   📅 Date: _____

Market Conditions	Available Funds

□ Options   □ Stocks   □ Forex   □ Futures   □ Crypto

Time	Name	Quantity	Buy/Sell	Price	Cost	Profit/Loss	Balance

Target / Stop :	

TRADING LOGBOOK

○ Mon ○ Tue ○ Wed ○ Thu ○ Fri ○ Sat ○ Sun 📅 Date : ....

Market Conditions	Available Funds

☐ Options ☐ Stocks ☐ Forex ☐ Futures ☐ Crypto

Time	Name	Quantity	Buy/Sell	Price	Cost	Profit/Loss	Balance

Target / Stop :	

TRADING LOGBOOK

○ Mon ○ Tue ○ Wed ○ Thu ○ Fri ○ Sat ○ Sun 📅 Date :

Market Conditions

Available Funds

☐ Options ☐ Stocks ☐ Forex ☐ Futures ☐ Crypto

Time	Name	Quantity	Buy/Sell	Price	Cost	Profit/Loss	Balance

Target / Stop :	

TRADING LOGBOOK

○ Mon ○ Tue ○ Wed ○ Thu ○ Fri ○ Sat ○ Sun 📅 Date : _____

Market Conditions	Available Funds

☐ Options   ☐ Stocks   ☐ Forex   ☐ Futures   ☐ Crypto

Time	Name	Quantity	Buy/Sell	Price	Cost	Profit/Loss	Balance

Target / Stop :	

TRADING LOGBOOK

○ Mon ○ Tue ○ Wed ○ Thu ○ Fri ○ Sat ○ Sun 📅 Date: _____

Market Conditions	Available Funds

☐ Options   ☐ Stocks   ☐ Forex   ☐ Futures   ☐ Crypto

Time	Name	Quantity	Buy/Sell	Price	Cost	Profit/Loss	Balance

Target / Stop :	

TRADING LOGBOOK

○ Mon ○ Tue ○ Wed ○ Thu ○ Fri ○ Sat ○ Sun 📅 Date : ....

Market Conditions	Available Funds

☐ Options   ☐ Stocks   ☐ Forex   ☐ Futures   ☐ Crypto

Time	Name	Quantity	Buy/Sell	Price	Cost	Profit/Loss	Balance

Target / Stop :	

TRADING LOGBOOK

○ Mon ○ Tue ○ Wed ○ Thu ○ Fri ○ Sat ○ Sun 📅 Date : _____

Market Conditions	Available Funds

☐ Options ☐ Stocks ☐ Forex ☐ Futures ☐ Crypto

Time	Name	Quantity	Buy/Sell	Price	Cost	Profit/Loss	Balance

Target / Stop :	

TRADING LOGBOOK

○ Mon ○ Tue ○ Wed ○ Thu ○ Fri ○ Sat ○ Sun 📅 Date : _____

Market Conditions	Available Funds

☐ Options   ☐ Stocks   ☐ Forex   ☐ Futures   ☐ Crypto

Time	Name	Quantity	Buy/Sell	Price	Cost	Profit/Loss	Balance

Target / Stop :	

TRADING LOGBOOK

○ Mon ○ Tue ○ Wed ○ Thu ○ Fri ○ Sat ○ Sun 🗓 Date :

Market Conditions	Available Funds

☐ Options ☐ Stocks ☐ Forex ☐ Futures ☐ Crypto

Time	Name	Quantity	Buy/Sell	Price	Cost	Profit/Loss	Balance

Target / Stop :	

TRADING LOGBOOK

○ Mon ○ Tue ○ Wed ○ Thu ○ Fri ○ Sat ○ Sun 🗓 Date : ....

Market Conditions	Available Funds

☐ Options   ☐ Stocks   ☐ Forex   ☐ Futures   ☐ Crypto

Time	Name	Quantity	Buy/Sell	Price	Cost	Profit/Loss	Balance

Target / Stop :	

TRADING LOGBOOK

○ Mon ○ Tue ○ Wed ○ Thu ○ Fri ○ Sat ○ Sun 📅 Date : ....

Market Conditions	Available Funds

☐ Options   ☐ Stocks   ☐ Forex   ☐ Futures   ☐ Crypto

Time	Name	Quantity	Buy/Sell	Price	Cost	Profit/Loss	Balance

Target / Stop :	

TRADING LOGBOOK

○ Mon ○ Tue ○ Wed ○ Thu ○ Fri ○ Sat ○ Sun 📅 Date : ....

Market Conditions	Available Funds

☐ Options ☐ Stocks ☐ Forex ☐ Futures ☐ Crypto

Time	Name	Quantity	Buy/Sell	Price	Cost	Profit/Loss	Balance

Target / Stop :	

TRADING LOGBOOK

○ Mon ○ Tue ○ Wed ○ Thu ○ Fri ○ Sat ○ Sun 🗓 Date : ....

Market Conditions	Available Funds

☐ Options ☐ Stocks ☐ Forex ☐ Futures ☐ Crypto

Time	Name	Quantity	Buy/Sell	Price	Cost	Profit/Loss	Balance

Target / Stop :	

TRADING LOGBOOK

○ Mon ○ Tue ○ Wed ○ Thu ○ Fri ○ Sat ○ Sun 📅 Date :

Market Conditions	Available Funds

☐ Options ☐ Stocks ☐ Forex ☐ Futures ☐ Crypto

Time	Name	Quantity	Buy/Sell	Price	Cost	Profit/Loss	Balance

Target / Stop :	

TRADING LOGBOOK

○ Mon ○ Tue ○ Wed ○ Thu ○ Fri ○ Sat ○ Sun 📅 Date : _____

Market Conditions	Available Funds

□ Options   □ Stocks   □ Forex   □ Futures   □ Crypto

Time	Name	Quantity	Buy/Sell	Price	Cost	Profit/Loss	Balance

Target / Stop :	

# NOTES

 NOTES

# NOTES

NOTES

NOTES